The "Knotty" Macrame & Beading Book

INTERSTELLAR

TRADING & PUBLISHING COMPANY

LA MESA, CALIFORNIA

ISBN 0-9645957-4-5
LIBRARY OF CONGRESS CATALOG CARD NUMBER 95-95203
SAN: 298-5829

All illustrations by Wendy Simpson Conner
Color Photography by Don Brandos
Printed in the United States of America

FIRST PRINTING: APRIL, 1996
SECOND PRINTING: AUGUST, 1996
THIRD PRINTING: JUNE, 1997

ACKNOWLEDGMENTS:
To Jennie, Priscilla, Joni and Paul;
and everyone who bought and loved
THE BEST LITTLE BEADING BOOK,
THE BEADED LAMPSHADE BOOK,
&
THE MAGICAL BEADED MEDICINE BAG BOOK

Introduction

Way back when, in another century (or was it in another life!) people knotted almost any type of cording they could find, and they called it "Macrame". They would sit, knotting away for hours, on their Indian-print bedspreads, wearing their negative-heeled earth shoes, drinking "sun tea", and feeling "mellow".

Well, Macrame is back, in a wonderful, modern way. You see it everywhere these days - even on the most sophisticated people. Macrame has outgrown its "home-grown" image. Many designers have included Macrame jewelry in their latest lines - you see models on the runways wearing marvelous, imaginative pieces that are very hip, and they look great!

The wonderful thing about Macrame is that the projects work up so quickly, and take so few beads, that you can make your jewelry very fast (and without costing much for materials), and if you choose to sell them, you can do quite well.

One of the biggest problems with working on this book was the fact that I had so many things I wanted to include - I write like I talk (a little too plentiful, I'm told), and the pages filled up too quickly. I've included 16 projects in this book, and had to be satisfied with fitting the rest into an idea section in the back. But you see, that's the way Macrame is . . . like those darn potato chips, you can't make just one. You'll see . . . as you're working on one piece, an idea will pop into your head, "well, maybe next time I'll try this knot . . ." One leads to another, and pretty soon you'll have many projects to show for your wonderful creativity.

Feel free to experiment with knots and variations to the projects in this book . . . obviously, a choker can also be an anklet, a bracelet, even a tummy cord. Experiment with cords, too . . . there's no limit to the variety, and no two pieces are truly identical.

This is the fourth book in a set of 25 books called **The Beading Books Series**. I hope you've read and enjoyed the other books, *The Best Little Beading Book, The Beaded Lampshade Book,* and *The Magical Beaded Medicine Bag Book.*. As usual, I've tried to include lots of diagrams and explanations. I hope you enjoy *The "Knotty" Macrame and Beading Book,* and find these projects fun.

As always, I love hearing your wonderful comments. Please feel free to write me c/o The Interstellar Trading and Publishing Company, Post Office Box 2215, La Mesa, California, 91943.

Happy Beading! ™

"Me"

Table of Contents

DESIGNS

Types of Knotting Cords

There are many types of cords that can be used for Macrame. Almost any thread can be knotted. This leads to all sorts of confusion about what is best. Most of the time, your cords are interchangable as long as you stay with the same general weight. Obviously, if you substitute a thick cord for a thinner one, you'll have some definite size-difference problems.

Think beyond just your standard macrame cording. Below are some suggestions, but also experiment with what you feel will work best.

HEMP CORD - Derived from the Cannabis saliva plant (yes, THAT Cannabis), it's a rough cord that's used quite often in macrame. It doesn't stretch alot and has a lot of strength. The natural seal makes it water-resistant, so it lasts a long time. Unfortunately, it's hard to dye so it's usually left in its natural color. You may also hear it referred to as "sysal", "sunn", or "abica" cord, which are slightly different from hemp, but all derived from the same plant.

JUTE CORD - Derived from the Corchorus capsularis plant, it is one of the cheapest types of cording you can buy. This looks like a thicker, hairier hemp cord. You can buy this cheaply as packing twine at any office supply store (even supermarkets carry it). This is also left in its natural color most of the time, although burlap is derived from jute and is sometimes dyed (the fibers are finer in burlap and the dye "takes" better). The biggest drawback is that it deteriorates rather quickly with repeated exposure to moisture, so if you use this for jewelry, make sure you take it off before showering.

LEATHER CORDING - This is available in multiple widths, from 1/2mm to 3mm. The thicker the cording, the larger your knots will be, so experiment with the look you like the best. I usually use 1 mm - it's easy to work with, and holds its shape well. Leather cording is available in several colors: black, chocolate brown, natural light brown (tan), red, turquoise, gold, bronze, etc. For a really great look, try mixing your leather colors.

RATTAIL - This satin cording looks great when knotted - it's so shiny and elegant, it gives a very different look than the previously mentioned cords. It's available in 1 mm or 2 mm widths, and zillions of colors.

RAYON CORDING - This looks like a thick thread (it has a twist) and usually is fairly shiny. The biggest problem with this is the fraying factor - it does not wear very well as jewelry, but if you choose to use it for a plant hanger, fray out the tail (it looks like frizzy hair).

CONSO - A nylon thread that is used a lot for upholstery, it gives a finer look to your work. It comes in many colors, and you can even find one in that natural hemp color that's so popular. The conso is sealed, so it has a nice finish that really lasts. It's stiff when you work it, but it's definitely easier on the hands than jute or hemp. Use it when you want to use smaller beads or do finer knotwork.

COTTON CORDING - Super-cheap, you can pick it up at the drugstore. It's that white stuff that comes on a little spool that's sometimes used for packing and shipping. It does have the limitations of cotton (tendency to stretch or rot), but I used it for macrame projects 20 years ago that still look great (both of the plant hangers in this book were done with it, and I did them when I was 15). The cotton has a nice, polished look, and although I can't say I'd use it for jewelry, I think it's fine for plant hangers. Cotton doesn't last well when it gets wet alot, so if you do use it for jewelry, try to take it off before showering or swimming.

SILK THREAD - This is the same that you 'd use to string your necklaces and knot your pearls. Use "F" or "FF" weight - it is finer than the other cords mentioned, but if you use if on a watchband or smaller project, you can use your regular beads with smaller holes.

ELASTIC CORDING - You can actually knot elastic cording (1/2 - 1mm size) and have the best of both worlds - the enhancement of an elastic cord, and the ability to use macrame techniques that speed up your work time.

SOUTACHE - Another great cording, this one already looks like it's woven, and has a very nice look to it.

OTHER CORDING - As I always tell my students - treat yourself to a day at the upholstery supply store, or an office supply or fabric store - look beyond what your local beadstore has to offer (might as well check out the hardware store, too). Many great ideas and inventions came because someone went shopping and saw something new. You never know what you will find . . . just don't be afraid to experiment.

Knotting Cords Sizing Chart

ONE HALF MILLIMETER - Roughly
equivalent to silk thread, conso, etc.

ONE MILLIMETER - Leather cording,
rattail, elastic cording, some hemp, and some rayon cords, as well as several other types of cording are available in 1mm.

TWO MILLIMETER - Leather cording,
rattail, elastic cording, some heavier hemp, jute, rayon cording, some cotton cording.

THREE MILLIMETER - Leather cording,
jute, cotton cording, miscellaneous upholstery cording.

FOUR MILLIMETER - Miscellaneous cording

SIX MILLIMETER - Miscellaneous cording

EIGHT MILLIMETER - Unless you're
incredibly tall, I don't recommend using
this size cording for your jewelry. From here on down, this is for plant hangers or non-wearable projects!

TEN MILLIMETER - This gets a little
harder to knot when it's this heavy.

There are thicker cords than this available, but unless you really have a need to punish yourself, I suggest you stick to the thicknesses above. Don't forget - you can always use double cords to get the right in-between thickness.

Beads For Macrame

As you start working on your projects, one very obvious fact will jump out at you: you cannot put a really small bead on a really thick thread, unless it has a hole that accommodates the thickness of your cording.

This sounds so simple, yet so many times, you buy beads or cording that just aren't compatible with your design concepts. The best thing to do is to bring your beads with you when you're selecting cording, or your cording when selecting beads, and then you shouldn't have this problem.

Also (and forgive me, I know this, too, sounds so obvious), the worst beads for trying to macrame are freshwater pearls, seedbeads, and certain semiprecious stones that have not been drilled properly. Do pay attention to the way your beads are drilled: sometimes, within the same strand, you'll find great variations as to the size of the hole in the beads.

Sometimes, however, the beads fit just fine in the store, but when you get them home and start working, for some unexplainable reason, they just DON'T fit anymore. Here are some tips that should help you with that.

It's best to thread your beads on your cording when you first begin.

Now, this isn't always possible to do; but if you can, you'll be a much happier and less frustrated person if you can get your beads on your cording when you're just starting your project and the thread is fresh. If your design doesn't lend itself to this, keep a good pair of scissors (sharp) handy, and frequent trimming of frayed ends may be the answer to this problem. You can also dab on a bit of cement onto the ends to "clean" them up.

Humid weather will swell your cording

We're not the only ones who retain water - so do certain cordings. If you're experiencing problems with the way your beads are going on the cording, you may want to leave your cording in a hot car, and the (dry) heat should skinny it up again. Try to store your cording in a dry, non-humid environment, so that it will be easier to work with when you're ready (cotton is a real culprit when it comes to this).

Remember all those macrame beads with the large holes? All of those beautiful carved wooden beads that looked so great! Well, you can easily find those in thrift stores and garage sales for practically nothing - also try those beaded car seats that always fall apart - there are millions of wooden beads on those things - they'll last you forever!

Macrame Terms

Every craft has its own lingo, and macrame is certainly no exception. The following terms should help.

FILLER CORDS - cords that end up inside the knots.

HOLDING CORDS - cords with beads or other embellishments on them.

KNOTTING CORDS - used to form knots, these run vertically along the outside of the piece.

SINNET - vertical series of knots

HOW TO MEASURE YOUR CORDING

One of the most horrible moments in life is when you realize that the project you have worked on for days, and been consumed with the creation of, will run out of thread 2 inches too early! As you know, it is better to cut off and throw away thread then to end up short. This is one project that you won't want to be cheap about and skimp on your cording.

Everyone has a slightly different knotting technique. Some people make perfect little tight knots; some make big, loose knots. You will have to experiment to find your own true gauge. I can, however, give you a few basic guidelines to help you out.

Depending on the knots you're using, there will be times when you'll want all of your threads one length; other times you'll just need the knotting cords to be longer. When using the Square Knot, for example, if it's always the same threads that are making your sinnets, you 'll want the knotting cords to be longer.

A useful guide is to measure 8 to 10 times the length of the finished piece. If the threads are to be doubled (because they're being mounted with a half-hitch), measure this before you fold them over. You may want to start with this principle, then tailor it to match your own style. Also remember: the more beads you add, the fewer knots you make, so it takes less cording. I suggest that before you start any of the projects in this book, make a little sample piece to use as a gauge (just as you do in knitting); keep it for reference whenever you're using that particular type of cording and specific knotting techniques.

Other Materials

The actual supplies for Macrame are very minimal - a knotting cord, a few beads, and maybe an embellishment or two. It's the setting up to work that requires some thought.

The most essential item when doing Macrame is a good anchoring board. You can buy boards that are made specifically for knot work - they are a soft, kind of mushy cardboard that you can stick pins in to hold your work and they don't pull out. They range in price from $4 - $6.

There are other alternatives to this - if you go into the hardware store, a nice acoustical tile that fits the description above runs $1 - $3, depending on the size.

If you use the boards described above, you'll also need pins to hold everything down - "T" pins or dressmaker pins are fine. It's best if you use a larger pin, rather than a regular headpin, because it will hold tighter and anchor better.

Also, a clip board works well in place of a knotting board - I have one that I got at a garage sale for 25¢ - it's one of my most valuable tools! This travels well in the car, and you won't have to worry about losing pins. It fits into a large zip-lock bag, and is perfect for smaller projects. You can use the clip part to hold the beginning, and scotch tape to hold your filler cords in place as you work.

A good sharp scissors is a necessity - if you use an old dull pair, it will chew up your cording, and it may not end up looking as nice as you'd like it to. There are times when you'll need a nice, fresh end so that a bead will fit on easily.

It's a good idea to cement your beginning and ending knots - otherwise, they could roll out. Use a watchmaker's cement for this - you won't need anything too heavy-duty, just something that absorbs easily into the fibers and holds.

A button can be used for a clasp (please see the *"Happy Endings"* on page 50). You can also think about using unusual embellishments in your work. Crystal beads can be used, as can earring parts, curtain rings, "chicken" rings (remember those!), coins, wooden beads . . . in short, anything you want to incorporate will be wonderful.

Your work will run alot faster and without a lot of frustration if you follow a few helpful hints:

Always knot towards yourself.   Anchor the piece firmly, and work your knots in the way that seems most natural.

Anchor as needed.   It may look like someones biology experiment with all those pins, but you'll spare yourself the frustration of not having to deal with something that flops around like a fish. Just be careful not to pierce anything too critical with those pins - it could cause fraying in your cording. Try to place your pins in the center of knots, not in the cording itself.

Assemble your materials before you begin.   If you're making up your own pattern, or even following any in the book, it sometimes doesn't work to try to add a buckle or ring as a clasp after your knotwork is done. This is especially true if you're using the Half Hitch knot to start. There are ways of adding these things in later, but you'll end up having to use jumprings or wire, and that might take away from your design.

Protect your cording when you're not working on the project.   If you start a project, and halfway through it gets rained on, or the dog plays with it, etc., this will radically alter the way the piece finishes. Your beginning half will have nice cording, and your ending half may look kind of ratty if the cording frays.

Keep out of sunlight for the same reason - if the cording is not colorfast, there could be variations. Keep it protected in a plastic ziplock bag, or, if working on a large knotting board, use a pillowcase if you need to transport it.

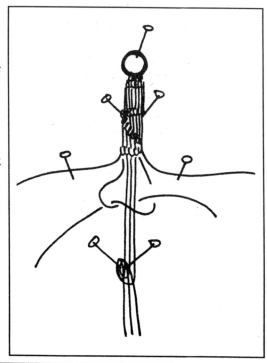

Color Photo Index

Not shown in color: Plant Hanger Number One and Knotted Watchband.

Macrame Knots

Here are the knots that will become your mainstay! Some of these are so important, that you will use them in every project. Some you will use less often but you will find them equally valuable.

THE HALF HITCH (LARK'S HEAD)

(USED FOR CONNECTING & BEGINNING)

THE CLOVE HITCH

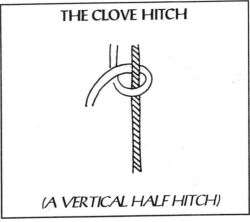

(A VERTICAL HALF HITCH)

ALTERNATE HALF HITCH

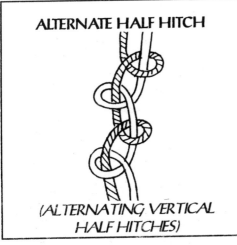

(ALTERNATING VERTICAL HALF HITCHES)

THE HORIZONTAL WRAP

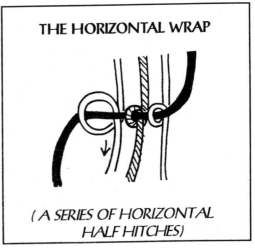

(A SERIES OF HORIZONTAL HALF HITCHES)

THE VERTICAL WRAP

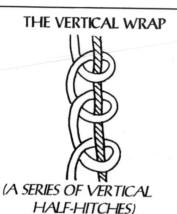

(A SERIES OF VERTICAL HALF-HITCHES)

THE DIAGONAL WRAP

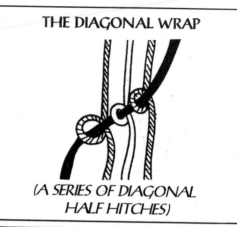

(A SERIES OF DIAGONAL HALF HITCHES)

BUTTONHOLE BEND

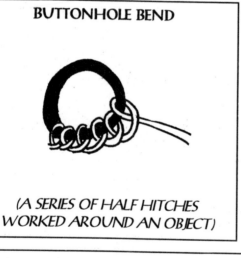

(A SERIES OF HALF HITCHES WORKED AROUND AN OBJECT)

THE BOX HITCH

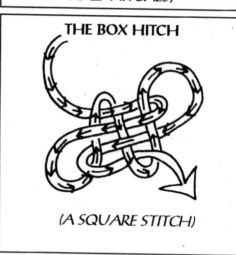

(A SQUARE STITCH)

THE JOSEPHINE KNOT

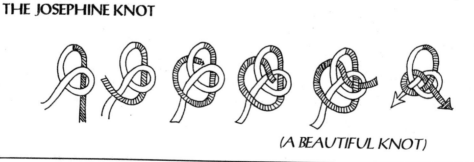

(A BEAUTIFUL KNOT)

THE HALF KNOT

(LIKE TYING YOUR SHOE)

THE SQUARE KNOT

(ALSO KNOWN AS A REEF KNOT, IT CONSISTS OF 2 HALF KNOTS, WORKED RIGHT OVER LEFT, THEN LEFT OVER RIGHT).

THE GRANNY KNOT

(LIKE THE SQUARE KNOT, BUT IT'S WORKED RIGHT OVER RIGHT, OR LEFT OVER LEFT. THIS CREATES A 'TWIST' IN THE SINNET.)

ALTERNATING SQUARE KNOT

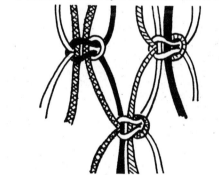

(MAKES A BASKET-WEAVE EFFECT)

THE BRAID

(ALSO KNOWN AS "PLAITING")

THE DOUBLE BRAID

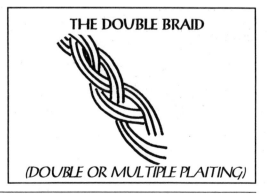

(DOUBLE OR MULTIPLE PLAITING)

"WHIPPING"

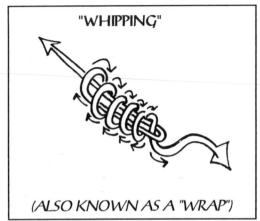

(ALSO KNOWN AS A "WRAP")

FIGURE "8"

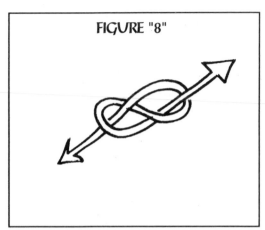

SLIPKNOT

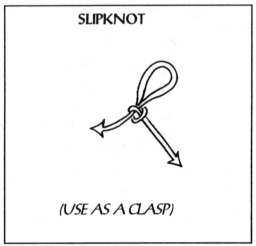

(USE AS A CLASP)

SHEEPSHANK KNOT

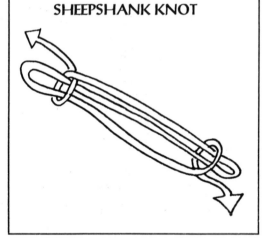

CHAIN KNOT

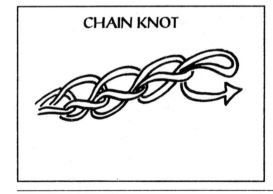

OVERHAND KNOT

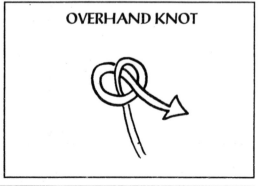

KNOTTED LEATHER BRACELET

This is such an amazingly simple bracelet to make, yet everyone you know will want one because it looks so great!

SUPPLIES NEEDED:
- ● Four yards of 1mm leather (for a bracelet - more for a choker or necklace)
- ● Use a pinboard or clipboard to hold your work

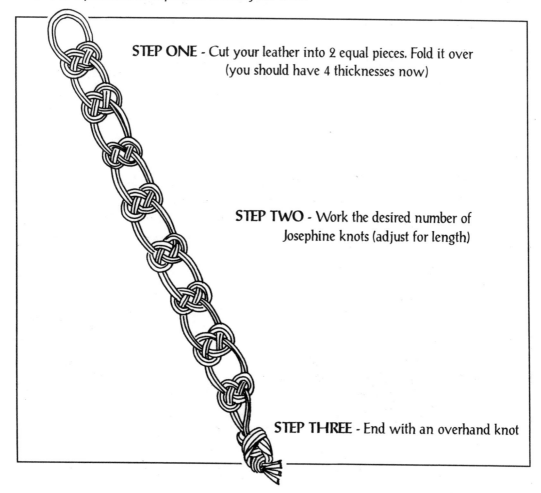

STEP ONE - Cut your leather into 2 equal pieces. Fold it over (you should have 4 thicknesses now)

STEP TWO - Work the desired number of Josephine knots (adjust for length)

STEP THREE - End with an overhand knot

KNOTTED ELASTIC BRACELET

This is a great pattern for children - it's easy for them to make, and it requires very little time or supplies. Being that it's constructed with elastic cording, and gets its shape from being tight, this is one project that I don't think it's a good idea to make as a choker.

SUPPLIES NEEDED:
- One yard 1mm elastic cording
- A variety of large-holed beads

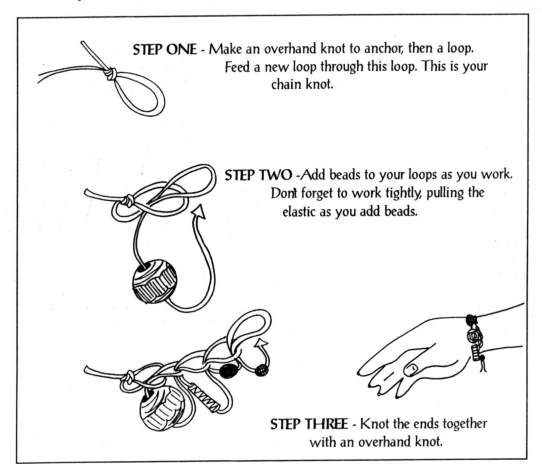

STEP ONE - Make an overhand knot to anchor, then a loop. Feed a new loop through this loop. This is your chain knot.

STEP TWO - Add beads to your loops as you work. Don't forget to work tightly, pulling the elastic as you add beads.

STEP THREE - Knot the ends together with an overhand knot.

The "Knotty" Macrame & Beading Book

TOGGLE CLASP BRACELET

You can achieve a nice variety of looks with this pattern. It can be elegant with crystal, or casual with other beads.

SUPPLIES NEEDED:

- Four two-yard lengths of green conso
- Six 6mm beads, one 8x16mm bead, and 14 silver heishi beads
- One toggle bar
- Cement

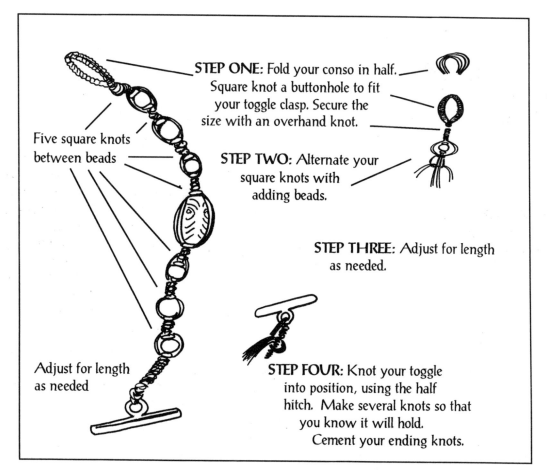

STEP ONE: Fold your conso in half. Square knot a buttonhole to fit your toggle clasp. Secure the size with an overhand knot.

Five square knots between beads

STEP TWO: Alternate your square knots with adding beads.

STEP THREE: Adjust for length as needed.

Adjust for length as needed

STEP FOUR: Knot your toggle into position, using the half hitch. Make several knots so that you know it will hold. Cement your ending knots.

This choker works up very quickly, and you can change the look with different beads.

SUPPLIES NEEDED:

- Six Two-ft. lengths of 1mm upholstery cording
- One 12" piece of 24 gauge wire
- Six 4x12mm rose quartz beads; twelve gold heishi beads, six pink glass rondells
- One buckle clasp
- One pendant; or a pretty bead and a head pin

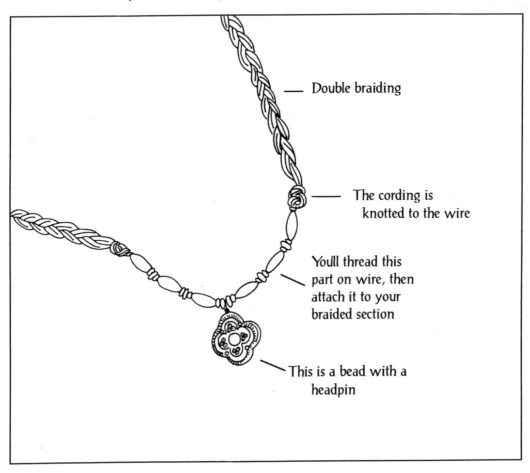

Double braiding

The cording is knotted to the wire

You'll thread this part on wire, then attach it to your braided section

This is a bead with a headpin

STEP ONE:
Thread your bead on a head pin,
make a loop at the top.

STEP TWO:
Take your #24 wire, and make a loop in one end.

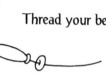

Thread your beads on in your
design pattern,
and add your
pendant.

STEP THREE:
Loop your wire at the other end, and attach your
braiding with a half hitch, then an overhand knot.
Attach 3 cords per side, each one folded over.
Braid your threads doubled (Three cords of 2 threads each).
Be sure that the threads lay nicely beside each other,
and do not twist. Work to length.

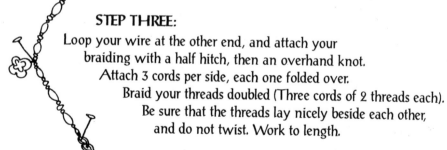

STEP FOUR:
knot your buckle
into place with an
overhand knot. Cement
into place. Repeat for the
second side. Adjust as needed for length.

BLUE CHOKER

When you make this choker, try to find blue beads that really make your blue thread stand out. The coloring in this one always reminds me of blue jays.

SUPPLIES NEEDED:
- One Chinese carving
- Eight 16mm beads
- One large 15x20mm bead
- Ten two-yard lengths of " F " weight silk thread

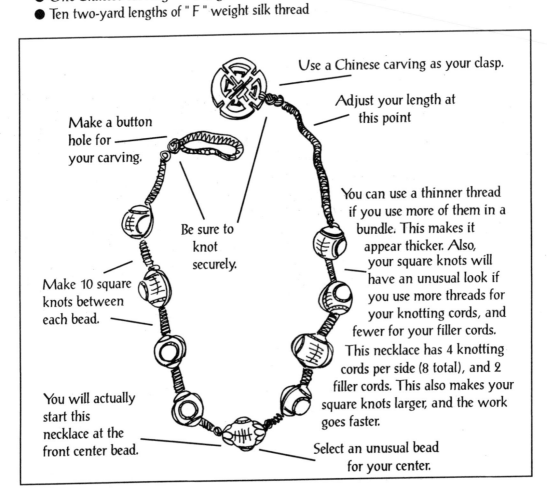

Use a Chinese carving as your clasp.

Adjust your length at this point

Make a button hole for your carving.

Be sure to knot securely.

Make 10 square knots between each bead.

You can use a thinner thread if you use more of them in a bundle. This makes it appear thicker. Also, your square knots will have an unusual look if you use more threads for your knotting cords, and fewer for your filler cords. This necklace has 4 knotting cords per side (8 total), and 2 filler cords. This also makes your square knots larger, and the work goes faster.

You will actually start this necklace at the front center bead.

Select an unusual bead for your center.

The "Knotty" Macrame & Beading Book

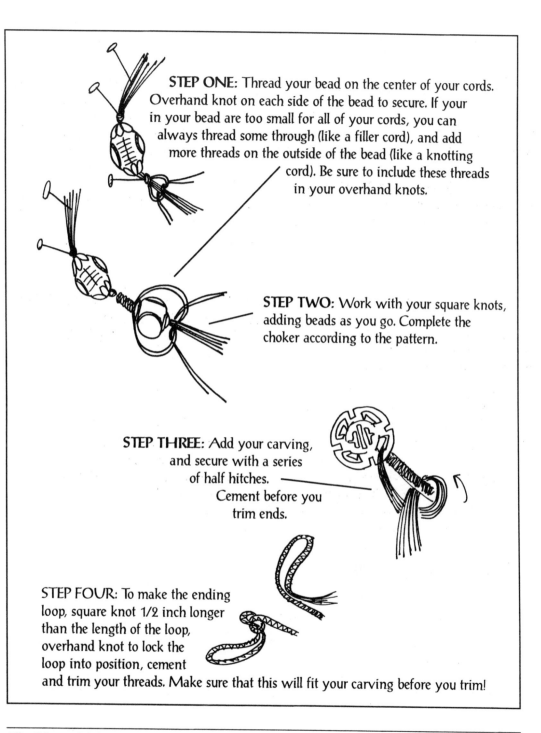

STEP ONE: Thread your bead on the center of your cords. Overhand knot on each side of the bead to secure. If your in your bead are too small for all of your cords, you can always thread some through (like a filler cord), and add more threads on the outside of the bead (like a knotting cord). Be sure to include these threads in your overhand knots.

STEP TWO: Work with your square knots, adding beads as you go. Complete the choker according to the pattern.

STEP THREE: Add your carving, and secure with a series of half hitches. Cement before you trim ends.

STEP FOUR: To make the ending loop, square knot 1/2 inch longer than the length of the loop, overhand knot to lock the loop into position, cement and trim your threads. Make sure that this will fit your carving before you trim!

CARNELIAN NECKLACE

This necklace opens up a lot more possibilities . . . now you can incorporate earrings, unusual findings, and other jewelry into your knotted piece. The carnelian pieces used here are actually earrings that I joined together.

SUPPLIES NEEDED:
- Three pendants or centers
- Four two-yard lengths of conso
- Five 10mm carnelian beads
- Two sterling silver 7mm beads
- Four black "E" beads

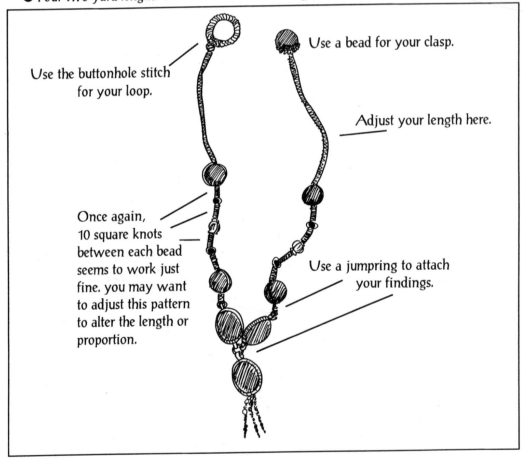

Use the buttonhole stitch for your loop.

Use a bead for your clasp.

Adjust your length here.

Once again, 10 square knots between each bead seems to work just fine. you may want to adjust this pattern to alter the length or proportion.

Use a jumpring to attach your findings.

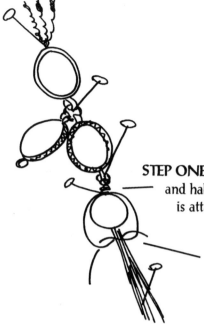

STEP ONE: Take two of your two-yard lengths, and half hitch them to a jump ring that is attached to your pendant. Make an overhand knot to secure.

STEP TWO: As described in previous patterns, alternate patterns of 10 square knots with your beads. You'll do the same with the opposite side.

STEP THREE: Continue on with your pattern. When you're ready to add your button, thread through at least one thread in opposite directions. Using your remaining threads, buttonhole stitch to strengthen. Keep your thread tight as you work, and you'll find it keeps its shape and works up quickly.

STEP FOUR: To make your loop for the opposite end, buttonhole stitch around your filler cords. Cement and trim. (Please do measure that this fits your bead/clasp first!)

The "Knotty" Macrame & Beading Book

RED CHOKER

This piece gets a little more intricate, because now we're mixing knots.

SUPPLIES NEEDED:
- Three four-yard lengths of 1 1/2 mm upholstery cording
- Six small pendants
- One large pendant

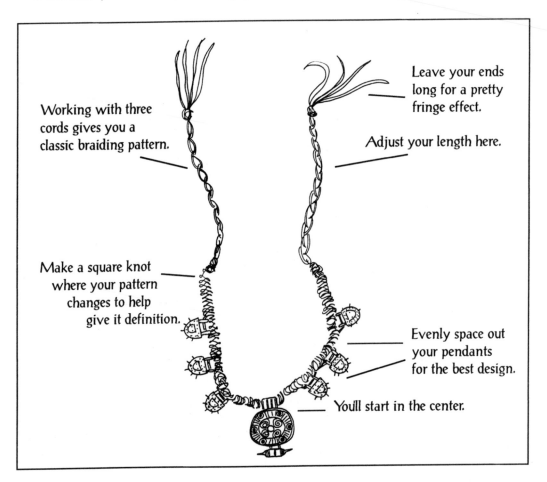

Working with three cords gives you a classic braiding pattern.

Leave your ends long for a pretty fringe effect.

Adjust your length here.

Make a square knot where your pattern changes to help give it definition.

Evenly space out your pendants for the best design.

You'll start in the center.

STEP ONE: Figure where the half way point in your cording is. Center your largest pendant here. If possible, run all three cords through the connector on the pendant, then make an overhand knot on each side of the pendant to stabilize.

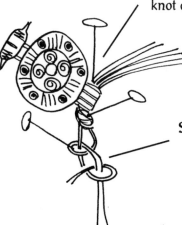

STEP TWO: Working each side one at a time, make your alternate half hitches. I made a total of 10 between each pendant (5 in each direction). The extra cord acts as a floating filler cord.

STEP THREE: As you add each pendant, pull one thread out, add the pendant, then continue weaving with all three cords. Try to pace it so that you're adding your pendant onto the odd cord, while you're making your half hitch knots with the other two cords. Then, just continue on as usual until you have your desired length.

STEP FOUR: After you've added the last pendant, work your alternate half hitches for about one more inch. Make an overhand knot, and continue the rest of the length with a braid. Make an overhand knot, and leave your ends long as a pretty fringe. Tie your ends at the back.

HEMP NECKLACE

This necklace is surprisingly easy to make. The hemp is easy to work with, and due to its thickness, it works up very quickly. You can also substitute Jute for the same effect.

SUPPLIES NEEDED:

- Fourteen assorted African trade beads
- Two two-yard pieces (if you add length, or adjust the design, you may need more)
- One large ornament to be used for a closure.

STEP ONE: Anchor your catch with a half hitch. Use an overhand knot to secure.

STEP TWO: We're back to our basic pattern: 5 square knots, add a bead, 5 square knots, etc.

STEP THREE: Use your buttonhole stitch to complete your clasp. Secure with an overhand knot. You can even twist your buttonhole stitch to give it a different look.

If you use a lot of beads, then you won't have to worry about running out of cording (in length), because you'll be making fewer knots. You can adjust the length and make it longer, if you change your mind after you start the necklace.

The "Knotty" Macrame & Beading Book

HEMP ANKLET

One of the nicest things about working with hemp is how quickly a project gets done. This anklet takes almost no time at all.

SUPPLIES NEEDED:

- Nine assorted "Skunk" beads
- Two two-yard pieces (if you add length, or adjust the design, you may need more)
- One ornamental button to be used for the closure

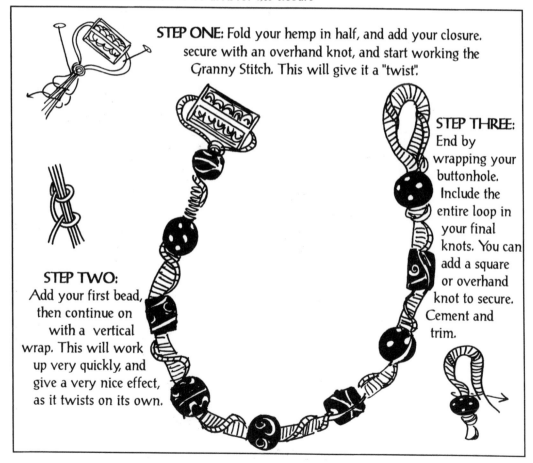

STEP ONE: Fold your hemp in half, and add your closure. secure with an overhand knot, and start working the Granny Stitch. This will give it a "twist".

STEP TWO: Add your first bead, then continue on with a vertical wrap. This will work up very quickly, and give a very nice effect, as it twists on its own.

STEP THREE: End by wrapping your buttonhole. Include the entire loop in your final knots. You can add a square or overhand knot to secure. Cement and trim.

LONG HEMP NECKLACE

This necklace has a very "earthy" feel to it because of the color of the hemp and the wooden beads.

SUPPLIES NEEDED:
- Sixteen assorted wooden beads
- Three two-yard pieces (if you add length, or adjust the design, you may need more)
- One button with a shank

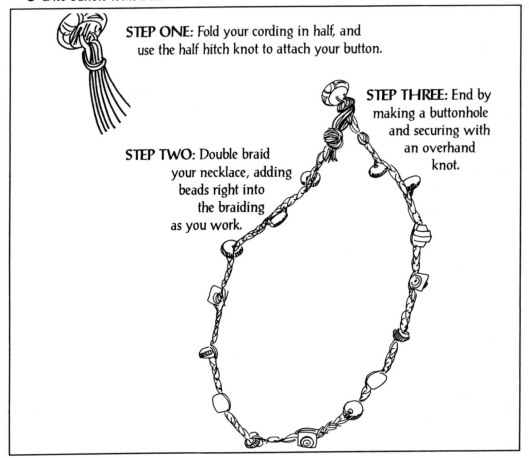

STEP ONE: Fold your cording in half, and use the half hitch knot to attach your button.

STEP TWO: Double braid your necklace, adding beads right into the braiding as you work.

STEP THREE: End by making a buttonhole and securing with an overhand knot.

TURQUOISE / PI NECKLACE

You can have a lot of fun with variations to this necklace. I've used smaller pi beads, however, you can use larger ones if you like, or combine it with heavier cording for a very different look.

SUPPLIES NEEDED
- Eight two-yard pieces of conso
- Six 8mm pi beads, and one 20mm.

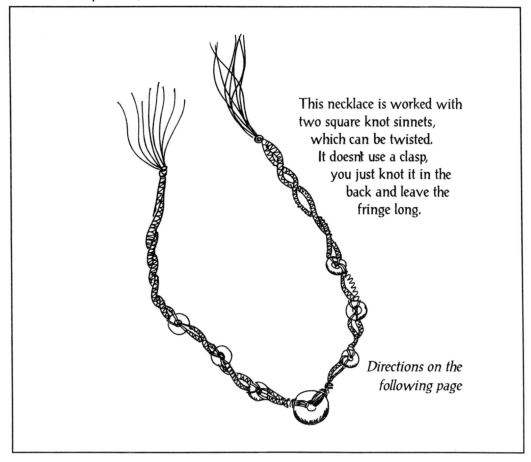

This necklace is worked with two square knot sinnets, which can be twisted. It doesn't use a clasp, you just knot it in the back and leave the fringe long.

Directions on the following page

STEP ONE:
Take four of your strands and fold them in half. attach your pi bead with a half hitch knot.

STEP TWO: You should have two groups of 4 threads each. These two groups of threads work independent yet parallel to each other. You'll work each group of 4 into a sinnet of square knots, with 2 filler threads and 2 knotting threads each.

STEP THREE: When it's time to add the first small pi bead (after about one inch or so), crisscross your threads through the hole. This will make the pi bead sit sideways, and not horizontal as it would by threading it on in only one direction.

STEP FOUR: Regroup into groups of four again, and make your two sinnets of square knots. Add the smaller pi beads at about one inch intervals. You can also adjust for length by adding or subtracting the length of the sinnets between beads. You can also add more beads, to give it a fuller look.

STEP FIVE: Work each side until you have the length you desire. Twist your sinnets together, and secure with a square knot. Leave your ends about 6" long, as this choker needs to be tied at the back. This will also give you a pretty fringe. Trim your ends even, and cement your final overhand knots.

FISH PENDANT NECKLACE

For this project, you need a large, dramatic, wonderful pendant. You'll be creating a thicker cord as you knot, so you'll want something that can "hold its own."

SUPPLIES NEEDED
- Four three-yard lengths of silky rayon cord
- Two large ceramic beads, and one large, glorious pendant

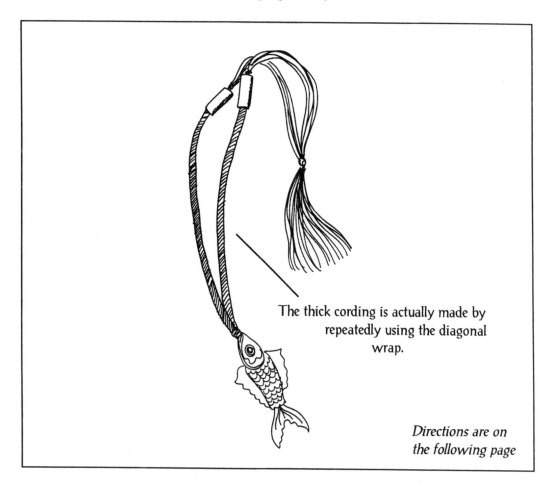

The thick cording is actually made by repeatedly using the diagonal wrap.

Directions are on the following page

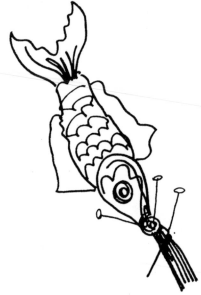

STEP ONE: Anchor your cord to your pendant with a half hitch. Make an overhand knot to secure.

STEP TWO: Now, you will repeatedly (and I do mean, over and over and over) make a diagonal wrap (a series of diagonal half hitches) that are completely parallel. About 5 inches into this thing, your eyes will glaze over with boredom, but don't worry - it's worth all this when you're done. Just keep going, and when you finish one side, you'll have the other side to work on also.
If you want your cording to have a thicker appearance, then double-wrap each vertical cord as its turn comes up. This can literally double the thickness.

STEP THREE: When you've had enough of this stitch, make an overhand knot where you ended, add one bead to each side, another overhand knot, adjust for length, and overhand knot the end. Leave a nice long fringe to add to the effect.

COPAL/HEMP NECKLACE

Copal amber is such a classic - it never goes out of style. This piece has a nice drama to it, because the copal mixes so wonderfully with the hemp and the turquoise.

SUPPLIES NEEDED
- Three large and two smaller copal beads
- Ten turquoise heishi beads and one pi
- Six large silver beads
- Six two-yard long pieces of hemp
- #24 gauge wire

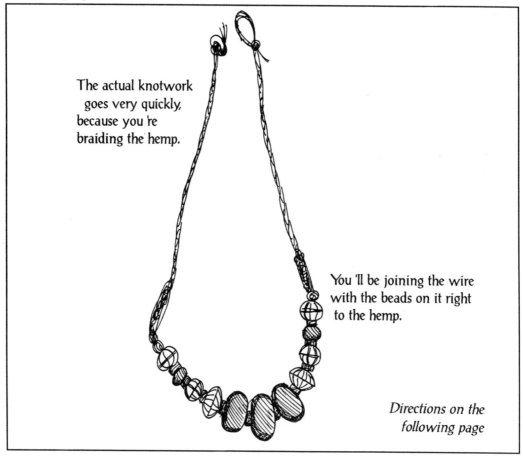

The actual knotwork goes very quickly, because you're braiding the hemp.

You 'll be joining the wire with the beads on it right to the hemp.

Directions on the following page

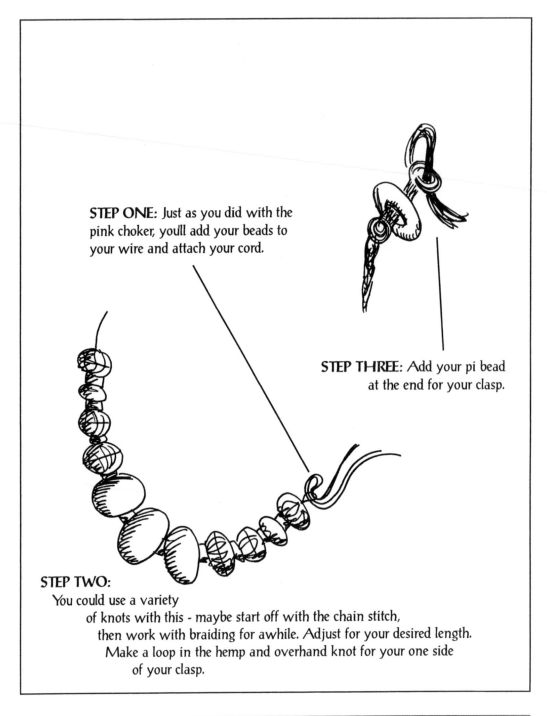

STEP ONE: Just as you did with the pink choker, you'll add your beads to your wire and attach your cord.

STEP THREE: Add your pi bead at the end for your clasp.

STEP TWO:
You could use a variety of knots with this - maybe start off with the chain stitch, then work with braiding for awhile. Adjust for your desired length. Make a loop in the hemp and overhand knot for your one side of your clasp.

MACRAME WATCHBAND

This pattern is more intricate, so it has more step-by-step instructions. Please don't let that put you off - it's a lot of fun, and you'll get a lot of compliments when you wear it!

SUPPLIES NEEDED
- Six two-yard lengths of conso cord
- Eight or ten tube-shaped glass beads
- One watch
- One small buckle

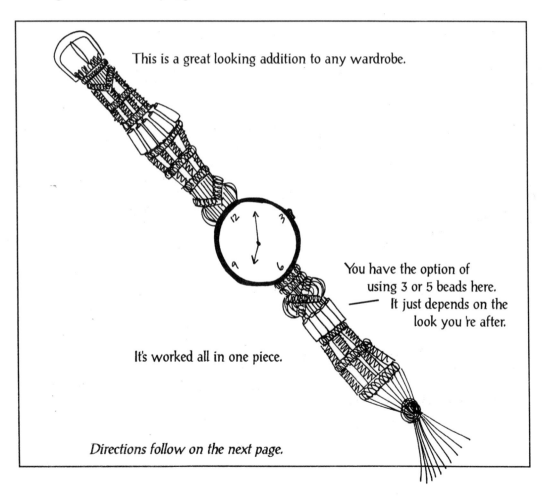

This is a great looking addition to any wardrobe.

You have the option of using 3 or 5 beads here. It just depends on the look you're after.

It's worked all in one piece.

Directions follow on the next page.

STEP ONE:

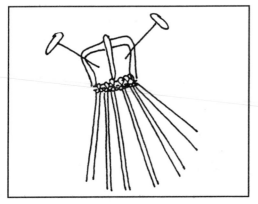

Fold your threads in half, and using the Half Hitch, attach 3 to each side of the centerpiece on the buckle.

STEP TWO:

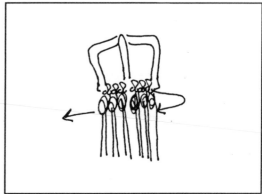

Anchor with a Horizontal Wrap.

STEP THREE:

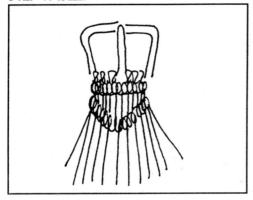

Using the Diagonal Wrap, bring the knots to a point in the center.

STEP FOUR:

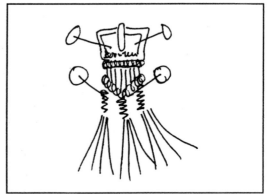

Divide your strands into 3 groups of four threads, and make 5 Granny Knots in each group. Make a Horizontal Wrap.

The "Knotty" Macrame & Beading Book

STEP FIVE:

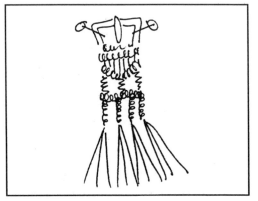

Now, redivide these into 4 groups of 3 threads, and make 5 Vertical Wraps in each group, as needed.

STEP SIX:

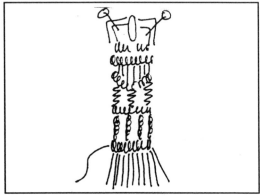

Anchor with a Horizontal Wrap.

STEP SEVEN:

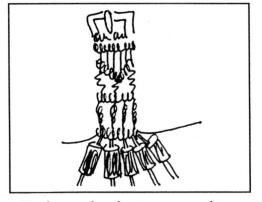

Divide your threads into 5 groups of 2, with one each left over on the outside. Add 5 of your beads to this.

STEP EIGHT:

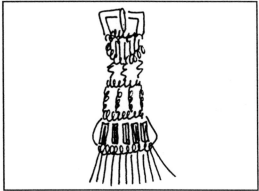

Horizontal Wrap just below the beads to secure them into place.

STEP NINE:

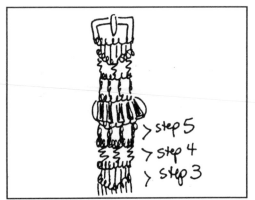

Repeat Step 5, then repeat Step 4, then
Repeat Step 3, then Repeat Step 4 again.

STEP TEN:

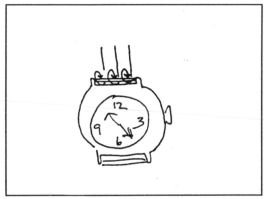

Loop your threads around the spring bar on the
watch. In the same way as you would
attach to a Horizontal Wrap. *(NOTE:
You may need to repeat some of the knots at
this point to add length)*

STEP ELEVEN:

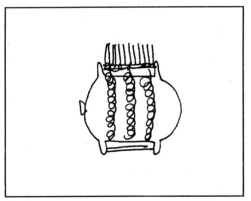

Divide your threads into 3 groups of 4,
then fill the back side of the watch with
Vertical Wraps.

STEP TWELVE:

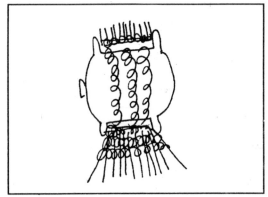

Repeat Step 13, and attach your threads to
the other spring bar on the watch.
Then add 2 Horizontal Wraps.

STEP THIRTEEN:

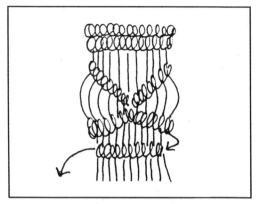

Crisscross 2 diagonal Wraps, then add a Horizontal Wrap.

STEP FOURTEEN:

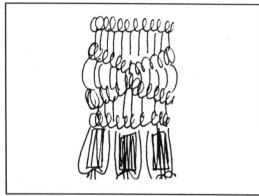

Divide your threads into 3 groups of 4; add your remaining 3 beads, then secure each group with a Granny Knot. Then Horizontal Wrap.

STEP FIFTEEN:

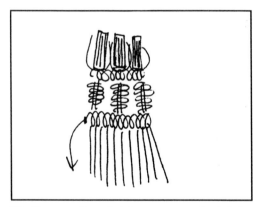

Divide your threads into 3 groups of 4. Make 5 Granny Knots in each group, then Horizontal Wrap.

STEP SIXTEEN:

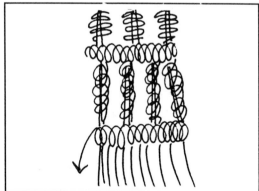

Divide your threads into 4 groups of 3 threads, then make 5 Vertical Wraps in each. Now, Horizontal Wrap.

STEP SEVENTEEN:

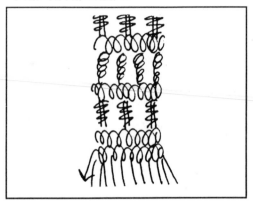

Repeat Step Fifteen. Then add 2 more Horizontal Wraps.

STEP EIGHTEEN:

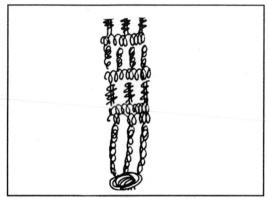

Add Vertical Wraps to the length you desire, then Overhand Knot all of your threads together. Cement and trim.

PLANT HANGER 1

Plant hangers are fun and easy to make. I made this one when I was 15. It just goes to show how some things are timeless!

SUPPLIES NEEDED
- ● Eight 2-yard lengths of 2mm cotton twine
- ● One 1" curtain ring

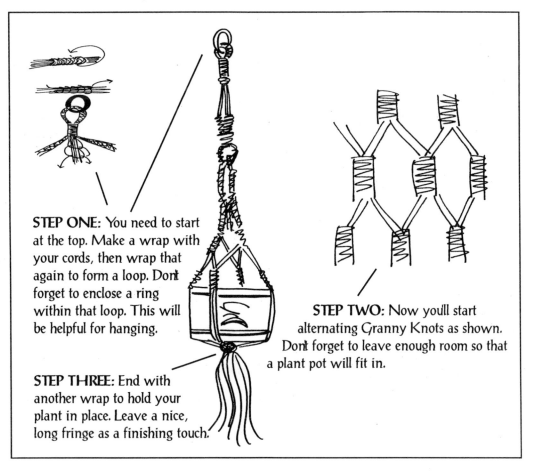

STEP ONE: You need to start at the top. Make a wrap with your cords, then wrap that again to form a loop. Don't forget to enclose a ring within that loop. This will be helpful for hanging.

STEP TWO: Now you'll start alternating Granny Knots as shown. Don't forget to leave enough room so that a plant pot will fit in.

STEP THREE: End with another wrap to hold your plant in place. Leave a nice, long fringe as a finishing touch.

PLANT HANGER 2

This plant hanger takes a little longer to make, but it sure is worth it! Work it on a frame that is usually used for moss, or any other framework, and everyone you know will ask for one!

SUPPLIES NEEDED:

- ● Fifty-six 10-yard lengths of white cotton twine ● One plant frame (10" diameter)
- ● One two-inch curtain ring

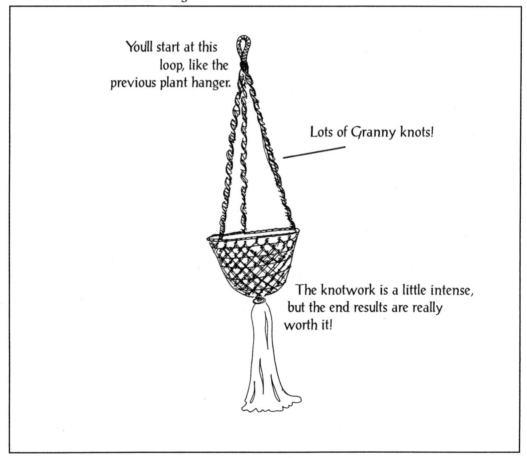

You'll start at this loop, like the previous plant hanger.

Lots of Granny knots!

The knotwork is a little intense, but the end results are really worth it!

STEP ONE: Starting at the top loop, fold twelve of your cords in half. Use the same wrapping technique discussed in the previous pattern.

STEP TWO: Divide your cords into 3 groups of 8. Work the Granny Knot with these cords to create your top section. The Granny knots give a nice twisting effect. Continue working until you have your desired length (about 18").

STEP THREE: Attach your 3 sinnets to the wire basket. Use half hitch knots and secure it well.

STEP FOUR: Now (you'll love this part) you need to attach ALL of those other long strands. Fold them over and use the half hitch knot. If you find there is the bare wire of the frame showing, you may want to fill in the gaps with an extra half hitch.

STEP FIVE: Continue to work by alternating your square knots to make a mesh pattern. Don't forget to weave in the wire frame as you work (wrap your cord around it). If your knots are overly tight, then you may need to add cording as you go. Finish by knotting under the wire frame when done, either with another wrapping knot, or a large overhand knot. Leave the fringe long.

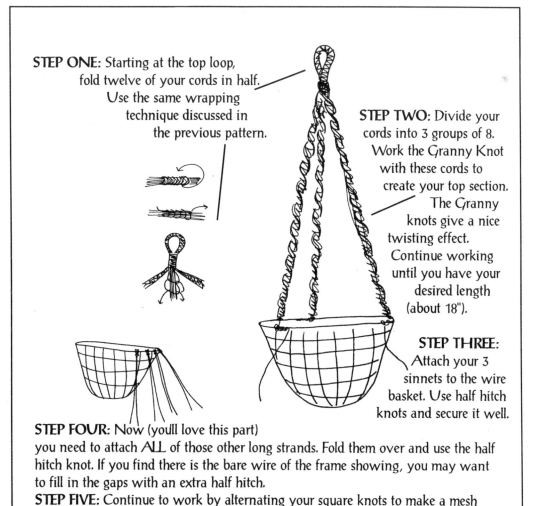

Other (Happy) Endings

Now that you've had fun with the designs in this book, you can really go to town with your own great ideas! Here are some suggestions for closures on macrame'd necklaces or bracelets:

● Use an end cone and wire. Wrap the wire around the end of your cords tightly. Cement and trim the edges. Tuck into an end cone, and pull the wire up through the hole. Attach to your clasp, just as you would a multistrand necklace.

● Use old buckles from doll's shoes, or old watch straps, or even small belt buckles for a clasp.

● Go to antique stores and find unusual pieces of old jewelry. Sometimes, you can buy a grab bag full of treasures for only $1.00! You can incorporate these pieces in with your macrame and make very elegant chokers for evening wear. Try rhinestones! They look fabulous!

● If you have old hair barrettes, or shoe clips, or even items from the hardware department, think of fun ways to use them in your jewelry!

So you see, the sky's the limit . . . there's no end to your creativity!

About the Author

Wendy Simpson Conner is no stranger to beads. As a third-generation bead artist, she grew up with beads from a very early age. Her grandmother was a jewelry and costume designer for the Ziegfeld Follies.

Being from a creative family, Wendy spent her childhood doing many types of crafts in a rural community. ("There just wasn t anything else to do!"). Over the years, she has mastered many techniques, but beads remained her first love.

She worked as a designer in television for awhile, and also has a strong illustration background (she always insists on doing her own illustrations).

Wendy has been teaching a vocational beadwork class for San Diego Community Colleges and the Grossmont Adult School District for over twelve years. She not only teaches beading technique, but also the dynamics of running your own jewelry business.

Her first book, *The Best Little Beading Book,* was the result of many of her classroom handouts. All of her books, including *The Beaded Lampshade Book, The Magical Beaded Medicine Bag Book, The Beaded Watchband Book,* and the *Jewelry for a Wedding Book,* have been very popular. They are part of **The Beading Books Series,** a collection of 25 books devoted to preserving beading techniques and history.

Wendy is available to teach workshops. If you are interested, please contact her through the Interstellar Publishing Company, Post Office Box 2215, La Mesa, California, 91943.

The "Knotty" Macrame & Beading Book

INTERSTELLAR

TRADING & PUBLISHING COMPANY

Other Books By the Interstellar Trading & Publishing Company:

● *The Best Little Beading Book* ●

● *The Beaded Lampshade Book* ●

● *The Magical Beaded Medicine Bag Book* ●

● *The "Knotty" Macrame & Beading Book* ●

● *The Beaded Watchband Book* ●

● *The Beaded Jewelry for a Wedding Book* ●

If you would like a list of other titles and forthcoming books from the Interstellar Trading & Publishing Company, please send a stamped, self-addressed envelope to:

**THE INTERSTELLAR TRADING & PUBLISHING COMPANY
POST OFFICE BOX 2215
LA MESA, CALIFORNIA, 91943**